# Words on a Page

Jenna Aleen

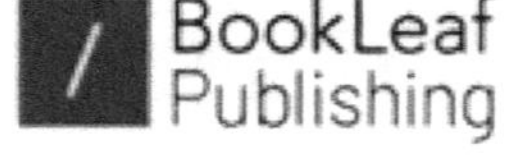

Presentation by *BookLeaf Publishing*

Web: www.bookleafpub.com

E-mail: info@bookleafpub.com

ISBN: 9789357210416

First edition 2022

# DEDICATION

To those who loved me, who broke me, who healed me, who changed me... I'm grateful to you.

May your journey be filled with peace, love, and healing

# PREFACE

The following pages are filled with the words I've never said, the words that have been said to me, and the thoughts that swirl in my head.

# Crawling

I hope you find the strength to stand on your feet
and be everything you desire and deserve to be.

If that's too much I hope you find a way to crawl
through the tunnel of chaos to the light at the
end.

On the days when crawling seems impossible, I
hope you just hang on.

# So I'm Not Dragged

It's an old saying, "let go so you are not
dragged."
The scrapes on my knees
The burns on my hands
They are the scars that make me beautiful
A permanent reminder of where you once were

# Crumbs

3

In the form of I'll be home in an hour, but
showing up four hours later.
Or the promise of sleep tomorrow.
The trail of breadcrumbs was always enough to
keep me coming back.
But never enough to fill me up.

# Wants & Needs

You said you had everything I ever wanted.
What you meant was "I am nothing you will
ever need"

# Chaos Is A Five Letter Word

5. For the way you looked at me
4. For the way you held me close then dropped me
3. For the things you said you'd change and didn't
2. For the list of other girls longer than I can remember
1. For the nights of worry

# Foreign Sheets

I lay in bed
I notice the sheets are wrong
The pillow is too fluffy
The noises of the room are foreign
The air is blowing ever so slightly, a plus I note,
but at the wrong temperature
The blanket is too thin but weighs the same as
the elephant that has made a home in my chest
My eyes close
All I see is you
I try to rest
I toss, then I turn
I have to sleep, I think
In this bed that I didn't make

# I Didn't Hear The Part

Keep going
Do the work
Walk forward and look forward

I listen while I glance over my shoulder

Some steps feel as if I'm walking on the shards
of a million broken glass hearts
Each step bringing another layer of protection to
my fragile soles

I glance back... its foggy now
Scabs are forming

Keep going
Do the work
Walk forward and look forward

My soles no longer bleed
I glance back... nothing
Nothing to see
Nothing to return to
A past vanished
A brushstroke equivalent to each step painted
over the picture

Keep going
Do the work
Walk forward and look forward

I want to run. Back over the broken glass hearts.
Wound my soles again. Feel it all twice It can't
be over I think. It is they say. I turn. It's just a
picture now. My soles healed. No longer
bleeding. Steps taken on lush forest beds, no
longer broken glass hearts.

Keep going
Do the work
Walk forward and look forward

I listened but I didn't hear the part where they
said
I wouldn't be able to go back.

# Broken Trophies Mean
# Nothing After The Fact

You put me on a pedestal. Up so high, cared for frequently, dusted regularly.

Like a shiny trophy that you won.

A prize gained through empty promises and broken dreams.

# The Moon Isn't Smooth

I'm made up of the moments of impact.
The imprint of the crash still hollowed out and
rough.
Cavernous and Treacherous.
A smooth touch along the edges and I cannot
hide the craters.

# My Apologies

To the people who made I made my homes.
Without knowing there weren't any windows.
Just four walls and a roof. There was electric,
just at the right times, flowing through us in an a
exhilirating way. A touch in the form of a spark.
In the worst days the water overflowed from the
pipes. You see when there aren't any windows,
you can't look out and home feels cozy. Until the
sparks create a raging wildfire, and the water
drowns you.

# Where Is Your Home...

It's been so many places

Here and there
And there and there and there

But is here really your home?

I hope it's home to you, I think to myself as I
watch you search for home everywhere else.
Home is where your heart is right?

He is home. He is home. He is home.

Someone tell him he's home I shout. The sound
of the can cracking is to loud, he no longer hears
me.

# The Sound of Midnight

13

midnight sounds like birds chirping in the trees

like the moon making the waves crash

like the stars that fly

# At My Door

You showed up at my door... cracked

Cracks showing from every catastrophic event
that has been the culmination of your life so far

Cracks created from every time you sought
connection and receivedA  coldness

Cracks from the promises of change that never
came

Cracks from nights of crying that never led to
calm downs

Cracked
Cracked
Cracked

You showed up at my door cracked but inside
you'll be coated in color

# Colors

Yellow - warm like the sun in the afternoon
when you long for a hug that will wrap you up in
a tangible warmth. Don't let go

Blue - the way the water looks gathered together

Clear - the way it is on its own
Clear - like the tears that run down your face

Anger oops that's the emotion not the color
sometimes it's hard to tell the difference - Red
like fire

Red Yellow Blue Clear Red Red Red
Black - blank - nothing. Are you there?

Orange like the color or the food. Food is a love
language I say as you peel my oranges.

# A Story of How I Went Down

Fall
Fell
Falling

# A Goodbye Letter

E for the events that lead me to the life we want
K for the way you knocked my walls down and
keep knocking on the days I don't answer
U for understanding you. You are a light. You
are amazing. You don't know it. I'll keep your
universe unique.
P for the way you picked up my pieces and gave
then gave me even more.

run it back

P for the way you put your hand on my thigh
with the window down
U for the way the universe works with an
understanding
K for all the kind words that smooth out the
cracks in the foundation that appear despite the
care
E for everything, everything, everything

run it back

add a D for the way I now demand the love I deserve. For the way to end it all. For the past tense.

puked.

# Who Talked You Off The Ledge

Your words are smooth and they soothe
Then they are sharp and leave shards
Words... They lead me all the way to the edge
The edge of the ledges I've talked you off so
many times
Soothing you without smooth or sharp words
Without the sharpness of a tongue like yours
Leaving no shards for you to walk over as I lead
you away from the edge

# The End

At the end of the day, the day will end.
And if we are ever so lucky, it will begin again
tomorrow.
Until then, may you be safe, may you be well,
and may you remember you are loved.